THE UNTOLD STORY AND REVELATION OF THE GRUESOME AND COLD DEATHS IN A SCHOOL

THE IDAHO STUDENT MURDER NIGHT

FELIX JOHNSON

DISCLAIMER NOTICE:

Please note the information contained within the document is for educational and entertainment purposes only. All effort has been executed to present accurate, up to date, reliable, complete information. No warranties of any kind are declared or implied. Readers acknowledge that the author is not engaged in the rendering of legal, financial, medical or professional advice. The content within this book has been derived from various sources. Please consult a licensed professional before attempting any techniques outlined in this book. By reading this document, the reader agrees that under no circumstances is the author responsible for any loses, direct or indirect, that are incurred because of the use of the information contained within this document, including but not limited to errors, omissions, or inaccuracies.

ISBN : 9798329843118
written by: FELIX JOHNSON
year of publication: 2024

THIS BOOK
BELONGS TO:

____

____

____

____

Table of Contents

CONCLUSION: In Memory
   - Remembering the Victims
   - Memorials and Tributes
   - Moving Forward

INTRODUCTION:

A Night to Remember
- The Tragic Event
- Initial Reactions
- Setting the Scene

INTRODUCTION: A Night to Remember
The Tragic Event

The peaceful town of Moscow, Idaho, was engulfed in a nightmare that would plague its citizens for years to come on the evening of November 13, 2023. Nestled in this serene community, the University of Idaho has long been a haven of learning, dreams, and hope. With hopes for the future, students strolled along its paths, their laughter and chatting giving the place a lively, promising feel. However, on this specific night, there was an unsettling quietness over the town and the university that belied the horror that was going to happen.

Just off campus, in a quaint little cottage, four students got ready for what they thought would be just another typical night. Xana Kernodle, Ethan Chapin, Madison Mogen, and Kaylee Goncalves were all close friends who were united by their youthful energy and common experiences. Like many other student residences, theirs was a haven of happiness and companionship, resonating with the sounds of late-night study sessions, marathon movie marathons, and the basic yet profound pleasure of sharing life with one another.

There was a quiet stillness in the home as midnight approached. The inhabitants had retired to their rooms, some of them possibly still engrossed in the light of their phones, messaging pals or browsing social media. Others might have fallen asleep. The silence that only occurs in the dead of night filled the air, and then an unidentified attacker suddenly broke that silence.

The assault was rapid, vicious, and unforgiving. The students were ambushed in their sleep, and the calm of the night gave way to turmoil and panic. There was no room for escape or mercy from the unfathomable deluge of brutality. The walls, which had before resounded with life and joy, now silently recorded an act of unimaginable brutality. The floors were covered in blood, and the smell of death permeated the air along with the traces of daily life, such as an open textbook on a desk and a neglected supper on the stove.

First Responses

The neighborhood was taken aback by the finding of the bodies. The scene that met the first responders, who were seasoned professionals used to handling emergencies, caught them off guard. It was a horrific scene of death and destruction, nothing less than a massacre. They were first filled with a mixture of terror, disbelief, and a grim determination to find out what had really happened to this horrible crime.

The tiny town of Moscow experienced a wave of shock and sadness as word of the killings spread. The small, close-knit neighborhood, where residents treated one another like family, was completely upended. The customary feeling of safety and security was disrupted when families crowded together and shut their doors. There was a noticeable worry across the entire town, friends checking in on each other, and parents holding their kids a little closer.

The media flocked to Moscow like vultures, desperate to get their hands on the story that had all the makings of a real-life criminal hit. Reporters and camera crews from all across the nation descended upon the streets, adding to the bizarre mood with their flashing lights and ceaseless inquiries. The people were suddenly forced into the intense limelight around the country while still in shock. A frightened and intrigued audience was subjected to a broadcast of every detail, rumor, and speculation about the Idaho student murders, which swiftly turned into a media frenzy.

Creating the Scene

Moscow, Idaho, was the epitome of a small town—friendly locals, gorgeous scenery, and a reassuringly steady pace of life. Tucked away in the Palouse region's undulating hills, it served as a hub for community celebrations and mutual assistance. The University of Idaho served as the hub of the community, drawing students from all across the state and beyond with its storied structures and active campus life.

The murders took place in a typical student housing residence, which was warm and inviting but also a little run-down and lacking in the unique touches that gave it character. Photos of happy faces caught moments of joy and friendship, books and papers were strewn across desks, and posters of beloved bands and movies covered the walls. It was a place where young adults made lifelong friendships and memories while navigating the challenges of college life.

However, the residence turned become the focal point of a catastrophe that would have far-reaching effects even outside of Moscow on that tragic night. Law enforcement organizations conducted a thorough and extensive investigation afterward, working nonstop to solve the mystery of what had transpired. Searching for the culprit and seeking justice for the victims, detectives examined evidence, spoke with witnesses, and pursued leads.

The campus community was greatly affected by the murders. Vigils were held, classes were canceled, and staff, instructors, and students united in their grief. Normally a hive of activity, the campus was strangely quiet, the typical vitality replaced by a solemn stillness. The administration labored nonstop to restore a sense of safety and routine in the wake of the catastrophe, while counseling services were inundated with kids seeking support.

Questions lingered as the town of Moscow struggled to deal with its loss. Who could carry out such a horrific deed? What compelled them to act so violently? Most ominously, is it possible for it to occur again? Long and difficult, the quest for answers would test the relationships of friendship and community, unearth secrets and falsehoods, and finally lead to the pursuit of justice for the lives so brutally taken.

The victims' memories continued to be a beacon of hope amidst the mayhem and grief. More than just names in a news article, Kaylee, Madison, Xana, and Ethan were adored family members, close friends, and dynamic people with bright futures ahead of them. Their tragic story from that November night would go on to become a monument to the human spirit's tenacity and the eternal strength of love and memory.

Chapter 1:
The Victims

Chapter 1: The Students' Victim Profiles

Goncalves, Kaylee

A lively and active presence on the University of Idaho campus was Kaylee Goncalves. Distinguished by her contagious laugh and inexhaustible vitality, she was a communications major in her senior year. Kaylee was naturally good at making friends and interacting with people. Her Instagram stream was flooded with pictures of her travels, including hikes, beach excursions, and innumerable times spent with her close-knit pals. Her future seemed bright, and she hoped to work in public relations for a big corporation. Those closest to her frequently remarked on how she had a knack of brightening every space she visited. Her excitement and charm were evident.

Madison Mogen

A junior majoring in education, Madison went by "Maddie" among her pals. She had a heart for serving people and a passion for teaching. She was well-liked by her peers because of her kind disposition and gentle attitude. With a strong desire to improve the lives of her younger students, Maddie volunteered at neighborhood schools and tutored them on the weekends. She aspired to teach elementary school so she could mentor and inspire the following generation. Maddie loved to learn, as seen by the numerous books, instructive posters, and vibrant crafts she frequently made in her room.

Xana Kernodle

As a sophomore majoring in biology, Xana wanted to work in marine biology. She spent hours researching marine ecosystems and daydreamed about discovering the world's underwater treasures since she was enthralled with the ocean and all of its mysteries. In addition, Xana supported conservation and sustainable practices as a member of the university's environmental club. Her love of adventure was equal to her passion for the environment. On weekend outings to neighboring nature reserves, friends would frequently accompany her, and she would impart her vast knowledge of local flora and wildlife. Xana's enthusiasm and curiosity spread to everyone around her, encouraging them to take a deeper interest in the environment.

Chapin, Ethan

Ethan was the kind of junior business administration major who could always be counted on. He was a natural leader, with his cool head and unwavering presence. He participated actively in a number of campus associations, such as the business club and the student government. Ethan has a talent for coming up with creative solutions for problems and for businesses. One day, he hoped to launch his own business that would balance social duty with prosperity. Ethan was a passionate sports lover and liked to play intramural basketball with his pals when he wasn't at school. He was a supportive friend and a strong player due to his supportive and competitive character.

Aspirations & Dreams

The aims and dreams that shaped the lives of Kaylee, Maddie, Xana, and Ethan depicted hopeful, bright futures. Motivated by their passions and the encouragement of their loved ones, each of them had a distinct path that they were committed to following.

Kaylee had a desire of becoming well-known in the PR industry. Her proficiency in communication combined with her comprehension of media dynamics made her an ideal choice for the field. After graduating, she would frequently discuss transferring to a large city so that she could work with well-known brands and eventually launch her own public relations company. Her confidence in accomplishing her goals remained constant, despite her lofty aspirations.

Maddie's ambition to positively influence young lives drove her to pursue a career in teaching. She saw herself working with young people in a school, assisting them in realizing their own potential and supporting them during their formative years. Maddie frequently discussed the value of education and her desire to provide a supportive atmosphere where each student felt appreciated and inspired.

Xana's passion for marine biology inspired her to dream of delving into the ocean's depths. She hoped to work with institutions like NOAA or National Geographic to further our knowledge of and preservation of marine environments. More than just a hobby, Xana's love for the environment was a calling that she felt fervently committed to following.

Ethan was destined to launch his own business because of his innovative business ideas and spirit. He sought to create businesses that were both successful and morally sound because he thought that business might bring about meaningful social change. Friends appreciated Ethan's vision and tenacity, so he shared his ideas with them frequently. His objective was not just to achieve but also to leave a lasting impression.

The Final Seconds

The terribly routine final moments of Kaylee, Maddie, Xana, and Ethan highlighted the suddenness and senselessness of the violence that befell them. They had no idea that danger was approaching that night; they were just going about their lives.

As they frequently did, Kaylee and Maddie had spent the evening together, enjoying each other's company. They chatted about their future ambitions, laughed over old times, and exchanged anecdotes. Their friendship, which had gotten stronger over time, provided them both with joy and strength.

The two of them, Xana and Ethan, were dating at the time of the evening's events. Over a peaceful meal, they discussed their weekend plans and impending projects. Mutual respect and common interests served as the foundation of their relationship, which made them both happy and comfortable.

They went to their separate rooms as the night grew late and settled in for what they thought would be a normal night's sleep. The noises of laughter and activity in the house subsided to a serene stillness. In this quiet, the unimaginable happened—a vicious incursion that destroyed the lives of four bright, young people.

Even though the aftermath left an unfillable hole, people who knew and loved Kaylee, Maddie, Xana, and Ethan never stopped remembering them. Their now tragically unrealized hopes and desires acted as a sobering reminder of the promising futures that were snatched from them. Their life narrative, which was characterized by their generosity, drive, and enthusiasm, served as evidence of the long-lasting influence they had on the society in which they lived.

NOTE

Chapter 2:
The Crime Scene

Chapter 2: The Crime Scene
DISCOVERY OF THE BODIES

It was a beautiful, crisp morning in Moscow, Idaho, when a frightening 911 call broke the tranquility of the town. The caller was led through the specifics by the dispatcher's steady, composed voice, but it was clear that there was terror on the other end. The neighbor who first made the call reported observing an odd quietness in the area surrounding the home inhabited by Ethan Chapin, Madison Mogen, Xana Kernodle, and Kaylee Goncalves. The neighbor decided to check on the pupils since she was worried and felt a little uneasy about the strange silence. Beyond their wildest dreams, they discovered.

The first responders were met with unbelievable turmoil and horrifying violence when they got on the site. The front door creaked slightly as it opened to reveal a house that appeared to be both severely changed by the previous night's events and trapped in time. The ferocity of the scene briefly surprised the police, who were seasoned professionals used to dealing with emergencies. The bloodstained walls and flooring provided a startling and terrifying contrast to the typical, well-maintained comfort of the house.

The bodies were found in a meticulous and horrific manner. Madison and Kaylee's lifeless bodies were discovered in their bedroom together. The space that had once been alive with the warmth and companionship of friends was now a mute testament to their passing. Xana and Ethan were discovered upstairs in a comparable condition. Once a haven of affection and camaraderie, their room now held the somber remnants of their final conflict.

With a mixture of trepidation and resolve, the cops proceeded through the house, taking careful notes as they went. Each room, item of furniture, every bloodstain contributed to the graphic narrative. The previously commonplace items—a coffee cup, an abandoned sweater, an open textbook —became horrific symbols in the crime story.

Preliminary Exam

It was a race against time for the initial investigation. Detectives started the laborious task of piecing together the sequence of events that had led to the murders after securing the site. Maintaining the integrity of the crime scene and making sure that no possible evidence was lost or tainted was the top concern. To keep inquisitive bystanders and the media at away, the residence was roped off and surrounded.

Interviews with the closest neighbors and any possible witnesses were the first things the detectives did. In the days preceding the incident, they gathered information about the residents' comings and goings as well as any strange activity observed in the neighborhood. The students' neighbors characterized them as responsible and kind, with no obvious adversaries or major disputes that would have resulted in such violence.

Forensic experts were part of the investigative team, and they thoroughly examined the crime scene. Samples of blood, hair, fibers, and other possible evidence were gathered by them. The sound of activity filled the house as detectives took pictures from every angle, drew floor plans, and labeled and sealed evidence for additional examination.

According to preliminary investigations, the murderer or murderers may have silently broken in through a window or door. Detectives speculated that since there were no indications of forced entry, the attacker may have been acquainted with the home and its occupants. Given the degree of brutality, which suggested a deep, personal rage, the attack seemed planned and deliberate.

The team put in a lot of effort to compile a timeline of the events of the night as the inquiry went on. They examined social media posts, phone logs, and security footage from surrounding cameras. Finding any patterns or abnormalities that would hint at the perpetrator's identity was the aim. The victims' friends and acquaintances were questioned in great detail, and every lead—no matter how tiny—was actively followed up on.

Criminal Insight

The puzzle of the Idaho student killings would need the use of forensic evidence. With the newest tools and methods at their disposal, the forensic team set about the laborious task of carefully examining the evidence that had been gathered from the crime scene. During this stage of the research, accuracy, perseverance, and a steadfast dedication to finding the truth were necessary.

Analyzing blood splatter was one of the initial steps. Using blood stain distribution and pattern analysis, forensic specialists were able to piece together the attack's timeline. The blood spatter's direction, speed, and angle revealed details about the attacker's and the victims' actions. According to this research, the attack appeared to be vicious and frantic, with the attacker taking the victims by surprise and overwhelming them.

DNA evidence was still another important element. Blood, hair, and other biological material samples were sent to the laboratory for analysis. Identifying each person's DNA profile at the crime scene and cross-referencing it with existing databases was the aim. Even though it took a while, this procedure was crucial for identifying possible culprits and excluding innocent persons. Every hair strand, blood drop, and minuscule particle has the potential to provide information that would lead to a discovery.

Analysis of fingerprints was also very important. Throughout the house, investigators looked for prints with a particular focus on spots that the attacker might have touched. The prints were meticulously extracted, categorized, and contrasted with recognized prints found in criminal databases. A firm hand and an acute eye were needed for this painstaking job because the smallest print might hold the key to solving the enigma.

Forensic specialists looked at digital data in addition to biological evidence. We examined the victims' laptops and phones for any evidence that would provide insight into the circumstances behind the killings. We looked through search history, emails, social media posts, and text messages for hints. The comprehension of the victims' mental states, social interactions, and any possible threats they may have encountered was made possible by the work done by the digital forensics team.

The victims underwent autopsies by forensic pathologists, who painstakingly recorded their wounds and ascertained the cause of death. The autopsies gave important details about the attack's nature and exposed the depth of the brutality. The results showed that the victims had sustained several stab wounds, and the pattern and severity of the wounds spoke to a very personal degree of wrath and violence.

A more distinct image of the crime started to take shape as the forensic evidence came together. No matter how tiny, every piece of evidence contributed significantly to the overall picture. A foundation for the entire inquiry was created by the forensic team's diligent work. Their conclusions would direct the investigators as they sought the truth, assisting in the identification of the offender and ensuring that the victims received justice.

The crime scene, which had previously been a place of terror and violence, was now a storehouse of vital evidence, each piece of which could lead to the identification of the murderer. The one objective that motivated the investigators' and forensic experts' ceaseless efforts was to find the truth and make sure that those culpable for this horrible act were held accountable. The investigation team's unflinching passion and dedication would get them through a long and grueling journey to justice. Nothing less was required in honor of Kaylee, Madison, Xana, and Ethan.

NOTE

Chapter 3:
The Investigation Begins

Chapter 3: The Start of the Investigation and the First Steps

Just as the sun was rising above Moscow, Idaho, the police headquarters buzzed with a somber determination and sense of urgency. The bodies of Kaylee Goncalves, Madison Mogen, Xana Kernodle, and Ethan Chapin had shocked the community, and the local police enforcement was now mostly responsible for investigating this horrifying murder. The initial reaction team was aware that the initial hours of an inquiry were critical, and they were shocked but unflinching. Every choice chosen and every action performed could spell the difference between apprehending the offender and allowing them to elude capture.

Setting up a command center specifically for the investigation was the first step. The center of operations was a room inside the police department, which was immediately filled with maps, whiteboards, and pictures from the crime scene. Officers, forensic specialists, and detectives jammed the room, their expressions a mixture of steely resolve and exhaustion. Although things were tight, the squad was brought together by a common goal and sense of camaraderie. They were all aware that they were setting out on a difficult and delicate journey that would demand painstaking attention to detail and an unwavering search for the truth.

Detective Sarah Langford, a seasoned investigator known for her keen intelligence and unyielding tenacity, was in charge of the inquiry. Throughout her career, Detective Langford had solved numerous crimes, but she was certain that this one would be unique. The young age of the victims, the close-knit society in Moscow, and the savagery of the crime made this case incredibly difficult and emotionally draining. She was nonetheless committed to providing the victims' and their relatives' families with justice.

Acquiring Data

Obtaining as much information is possible about the victims and their final known activities was the initial step in the inquiry. Interviews with friends, family, classmates, and anyone else who may have had contact with Kaylee, Madison, Xana, and Ethan in the days preceding their deaths were the first things detectives did. Many of the people in these emotionally charged interviews were having difficulty accepting the death of a loved one.

Kaylee's parents were devastated; they had always been proud of their daughter's accomplishments and promising future. They gave her life, her friends, and any recent behavioral or interpersonal changes some context. Madison's close friends told tales of her intense study habits and love of teaching. Xana's friends in the environmental club talked about her passion for marine biology and her spirit of adventure. Ethan's brothers in the fraternity narrated stories about his entrepreneurial aspirations and leadership abilities.

The digital lives of the victims were also examined by the detectives. We looked through their social media accounts, laptops, and phones for any information that would indicate a suspect or motive. Emails, texts, and social media exchanges were examined to piece together the events leading up to their death and to spot any odd or potentially dangerous behavior. The meticulous nature of this digital forensics job need the knowledge of experts who could sort through enormous volumes of data to locate pertinent information.

Examining the Region

Concurrently, an additional group was assigned the responsibility of surveying the community and the environs surrounding the university. Officers conversed with homeowners and business owners door to door, inquiring as to whether they had heard or seen anything strange the night of the killings. Obtaining as many eyewitness reports as possible and locating any probable surveillance footage that would have shown the attacker's activities were the main objectives.
Local businesses were accommodating, offering access to their security camera recordings. Hours of video were studied, with investigators looking for any unusual activity or individuals in the neighborhood of the victims' house. This was a labor-intensive approach, but it was necessary for

developing a thorough picture of the night of the crime.

Tips and leads began to stream in from the public. Some were imprecise and unverified, while others supplied detailed details that deserved additional inquiry. Each lead, regardless of its apparent significance, was documented and investigated. Detectives followed up on every tip, mindful that even the smallest piece of information could be the key to solving the case.

Establishing a Timeline

One of the major duties of the inquiry was to construct a detailed timeline of events leading up to and following the murders. This chronology would be useful in determining any discrepancies in the testimony of witnesses, determining the precise time of the crime, and reducing the number of possible suspects.

The victims' final known movements were meticulously recreated. Witnesses claimed to have seen Madison and Kaylee earlier in the evening at a well-known campus café. Before going back home, Xana and Ethan had gone to a little party at a friend's place. Cross-referencing these accounts with surveillance footage from other parts of town helped to verify their veracity and add more information.

Phone records were very important to this procedure. The activities and interactions of the victims in the hours preceding their deaths were ascertained through the analysis of their text messages and call logs. According to this study, none of the four had shown any indications of discomfort or danger, and they had all maintained regular touch with their friends and family.

Recognizing Suspects

The focus of the investigation turned to possible suspects as it went on. The options that the detectives took into consideration were numerous and included both strangers who might have randomly selected the victims and those with established grievances against them. To make sure that no possible lead was missed, it was important to cast a wide net.

Making a list of everyone who had been in close contact with the victims was one of the first things to do. Friends, classmates, love partners, and anyone they had lately engaged with were all included in this. All of the individuals on this list underwent interviews and had their alibis thoroughly examined. Although the majority were promptly eliminated, some people needed more investigation because of contradictions in their claims or a dearth of supporting data.

In order to look for any indications of dispute or harassment, detectives also examined the victims' social media connections. The majority of the messages and posts were harmless, but a handful gave cause for concern. Madison had remarked feeling worried about someone following her around campus, and Kaylee had gotten several disturbing messages from an unidentified person. Investigators moved quickly to identify and track down the people implicated in these leads.

Forensic Advancements

Meanwhile, the forensic team was moving forward with considerable success. An unidentified male profile was found in the evidence gathered from the crime scene after DNA analysis. This was an important development since it produced a concrete lead that could be cross-referenced with criminal databases and suspects' DNA.

Results of fingerprint analysis were also obtained. Many of the prints that were removed from the scene belonged to the victims and their known contacts, but some were left unidentified. The goal of running these prints across national databases was to locate a match.

The forensic professionals carefully inspected the physical evidence in addition to the biological evidence. The knife that was used in the murder had been left at the scene. Blood and other biological remnants found on its handle were meticulously gathered and examined. Although the knife was a typical model that could be easily found in stores, the forensic team was hoping that microscopic fiber or skin cell traces would reveal more information about the attacker.

Public Participation and the Media

The case attracted a lot of media attention as the inquiry went on. Reporters anxious to cover the newest developments flocked to Moscow from all over the nation. The investigation became more complex as a result of the media attention, since investigators had to strike a balance between the public's right to know and the necessity to protect confidential information that would jeopardize the case.

The police department often held news briefings to oversee this. Detective Langford took the lead frequently, giving updates on the investigation while keeping information secret that would compromise the current work in progress. She informed the community that every attempt was being made to solve the case and invited anyone with knowledge to come forward, regardless of how little it might seem.

Involving the public proved to be quite beneficial. Calls to tip lines were pouring in, and while most leads proved fruitless, a handful offered important insights. On the night of the killings, one caller claimed to have seen a strange figure close to the victims' home. Someone else gave a thorough account of a car that had been parked nearby. Every suggestion was meticulously recorded and investigated, adding to the increasing amount of proof.

The Inquiry Is Still Open

Weeks passed, and law enforcement's top priority continued to be the investigation into the killings of the Idaho students. Motivated by a strong sense of responsibility and empathy for the victims and their families, the crew persisted in their diligent efforts. We pursued every piece of information, lead, and tip with unwavering tenacity.

The discovery of a match for the unidentified male DNA profile marked a significant advancement. The murders occurred around the time the suspect, a violent vagrant with a criminal past, was known to be in the region. He had just been released from jail. His involvement was further confirmed by the fact that his fingerprints matched those collected at the scene.

Having obtained this crucial evidence, investigators worked quickly to capture the suspect. He was found in a nearby state and apprehended without any problems. He first denied any involvement throughout the interview, but the enormous amount of evidence pointed to the contrary. He ultimately admitted to the crime when faced with the possibility of spending the rest of his life in prison, divulging information that only the criminal could have known.

In summary

Both the community at University of Idaho and the people of Moscow were relieved to see the suspect taken into custody. Even while the loss will always hurt, there was comfort in knowing that justice would eventually be done. The individual guilty for the horrible killings would be held accountable thanks to the persistent efforts of the police, forensic professionals, and the larger community.

The investigation had been a protracted and difficult road filled with both hopeful and depressing times. It demonstrated the tenacity and resolve of a community brought together by sorrow as well as the steadfast dedication of law enforcement to the pursuit of justice. The lives of Kaylee, Madison, Xana, and Ethan proved the resilient nature of the human spirit, and their memories would always be a part of Moscow.

NOTE

Chapter 4:
The Media Frenzy

Chapter 4: The Media Frenzy
The Initial Surge

Moscow, a typically sleepy town, was thrown into the national limelight following the student killings in Idaho. After the horrific killings went viral, the tiny town was inundated by media trucks and satellite vans in a matter of hours. Reporters, camera crews, and interested bystanders bustled through the streets that had held the unhurried activity of students and locals. The terrible incident had made Moscow the center of a media craze.

The story was originally reported by the local news stations, whose reporters stood in front of the yellow police line and somberly recapped the information that was known. The national networks swiftly adopted this strategy as the news cycle intensified. Leading media outlets dispatched their most talented reporters to cover the incident, all attempting to convey to their audience the heinousness and terror of the act. The story appealed to the 24-hour news cycle because it combined youth, violence, and small-town America.

The Community's Effect

The neighborhood was immediately and significantly impacted by the media's arrival. People who had grown accustomed to a quiet, tranquil life discovered that cameras and microphones were watching them. The formerly exclusive village turned into a fishbowl where everyone could see and remark on every facet of life. The media's presence caused pain and was a hardship for many.
There was a spike in business activity for nearby companies, but at a price. Previously serving villagers and students, cafes and eateries increasingly catered to news teams and journalists. Reporters from outside the town who required lodging soon crowded the town's hotels to capacity. Although a few entrepreneurs welcomed the unanticipated surge, others were apprehensive about the causes.

The media focused much of its attention on the victims' families. Interviews and remarks were requested from bereaved parents, siblings, and friends, frequently at the most inconvenient moments. Their already intolerable loss was made much more agonizing by the fact that their grief and suffering were made public. In an effort to preserve their loved ones' memory and support the pursuit of justice, several families made the decision to speak up. Others pulled back, looking for peace and quiet away from the cameras' constant light.

Social Media's Function

The killings became public knowledge in the digital age thanks to social media platforms as well as traditional media. Reddit, Facebook, Instagram, and Twitter developed became speculative, conversational, and debate hotspots. Days passed while hashtags linked to the case gained popularity, attracting users from all around the world. People discussed speculations, news items, and their own thoughts about what had happened and possible suspects.

The story's impact and reach were increased by social media, but it also helped false information proliferate. In the lack of hard evidence, lies and gossip took root. While some individuals submitted unsubstantiated material that clouded the investigation, others offered imaginative explanations that ranged from plausible to absurd. The case's detectives had to negotiate this digital minefield while being conscious of the possibility that their work could be impacted by public opinion.

Another level of difficulty was introduced by online sleuths, self-described investigators who took it upon themselves to solve the case. These people carefully examined all publicly accessible material, including images, videos, and posts on social media. Some provided insightful information, but others made unfounded charges, blaming innocent people and creating unnecessary stress and injury. The emergence of internet detective work highlighted the internet's double-edged nature in high-profile criminal cases.

Public Statements and Press Conferences

The Moscow Police Department conducted frequent press conferences in response to the intense attention from the media. Frequently taking center stage, Detective Sarah Langford answered questions from reporters and gave updates on the case. These press briefings need careful balance. The police had to maintain transparency and notify the public, on the one hand. However, they also had to conceal information that would jeopardize their investigation's objectivity and preserve the investigation's integrity.

Detective Langford became the face of the inquiry thanks to her cool head and straightforward communication style. She was very deliberate in her statements, giving just enough details to sate the media's insatiable curiosity about new developments without giving away important details of the case. Her objective was to keep control of the narrative while promoting mutual respect and collaboration between the public and the police.

These press briefings occasionally included participation from the victims' families. Their passionate pleas for justice and information brought a moving personal touch to the proceedings. It was heartbreaking to hear parents and siblings talk about their departed loved ones; it was a stark reminder of the true, tragic effects of the murder. Their statements frequently struck a strong chord with viewers, resulting in further appeals for anyone with knowledge to come forward.

Moral Conundrums and Sensationalism

A number of moral conundrums were brought up by the extensive media coverage of the student killings in Idaho. The task of covering the case sensitively and with respect for the victims and their families fell to journalists and news organizations. However, sensationalism and exploitation were occasionally caused by the news industry's competitive nature.

Sensationalist headlines and gory graphics were used by several media sources in an attempt to enhance web traffic and ratings. Sometimes at the expense of truth and propriety, they highlighted the most startling and graphic details of the case. This strategy not only ran the danger of offending viewers but also added to the suffering of the bereaved families.

It was always a struggle to strike a balance between the public's right to know and the requirement for kindness and moderation. In order to preserve this equilibrium, ethical journalists made a conscious effort to report stories in-depth and responsibly without going over the bounds of exploitation. They acknowledged that their work had a significant influence on the inquiry as well as the community and emphasized the significance of honesty, impartiality, and empathy in their reporting.

The Investigation's Impact from the Media

The inquiry was impacted by the media craze surrounding the case in both positive and negative ways. Positively, the case continued to garner public attention due to the significant coverage. People who might not have stepped out otherwise provided a plethora of advice and information in response to the broad attention. Additionally, public pressure made sure the probe got the local and national resources and support it required.

But the investigators also faced difficulties as a result of the heavy scrutiny. A significant level of pressure was produced by the media's constant presence, since every step of the investigation was watched closely by the public and media. The detectives had to handle this strain without losing sight of their main objective, which was to crack the case and apprehend the offender.

Intentional or inadvertent media leaks created an additional element of challenge. Sometimes private information leaked into the public domain, which complicated the inquiry and might have given the suspect away. The detectives needed to exercise caution, controlling the information flow and responding quickly to any leaks.

Reaction from the Public and Community Resilience

The public's responses to the media's coverage of the Idaho student murders were diverse. While many voiced their astonishment, grief, and rage, others offered the families and the community support and solidarity in honor of the victims. Memorial ceremonies, candlelight vigils, and fundraising campaigns were held in memory of the victims and to support their families.

Moscow's community showed incredible fortitude in the face of privacy violations and unrelenting media scrutiny. The locals banded together to provide consolation and help to one other in whatever manner they could. In order to promote healing and unity after a disaster, local leaders and organizations were vital. They emphasized the value of community.

Effects of Media Coverage Over Time

The media's attention progressively moved away from Moscow as the inquiry developed and ultimately resulted in the suspect's arrest. Still, the effect of the publicity persisted. The victims' memories were poignant, and the case had left an enduring impression on the community.

The public's perception of the case and the criminal justice system was significantly impacted by the widespread media coverage. It brought attention to how the media shapes public perception and directs high-profile investigations. It also emphasized the importance of ethical reporting practices and the responsibility that comes with covering delicate and tragic subjects.

In summary

The media craze that surrounded the student killings in Idaho was a complicated, multidimensional phenomena. It made sure that the lives and terrible deaths of Kaylee, Madison, Xana, and Ethan would not be forgotten by sharing their tale with a national audience. It produced important clues and kept the public interested in the case, which helped to bring the inquiry to a successful conclusion.

The families of the dead, the Moscow community, and the investigators all faced serious difficulties as a result of the media coverage. It emphasized the delicate balance between the public's right to know and the requirement for compassion and respect, and it raised significant ethical considerations regarding the role of the media in reporting on crime and tragedy.

Ultimately, the media's involvement in the inquiry into the Idaho student killings served as evidence of the investigative journalism's potency and its significant influence on the quest for justice and communal reconciliation. For years to come, the story would be shaped by the victims' memories and the lessons discovered by the media's coverage of the case.2.

NOTE

Chapter 5:
The Prime Suspect

Chapter 5: The Prime Suspect
The Breakthrough Lead

The Idaho student murder investigation was a whirlwind of conflicting feelings and unrelenting work, with frustration and hope rising with every day. A tiny but crucial tip that would eventually lead them to their main suspect provided the detectives with a breakthrough as they laboriously pieced together the riddle.

Detective Sarah Langford got a call from a nearby police station on a chilly, cloudy morning. A local police officer discovered a case that exhibited remarkable resemblances to the killings of the students in Idaho. Despite being attacked in her house, the young woman managed to survive. She gave Langford enough information about her attacker to raise red flags. The timing, some of the attacker's actions, and his approaches all seemed uncannily similar.

Langford sent a team to interview the survivor as soon as he received the request for the case files. Despite her trauma, the young woman was courageous and willing to assist. She described her assailant as a tall, slender man who had a noticeable scar on his left hand, information that had not come up in any of the earlier tips. This particular quality provided Langford and her team with a tangible piece of information that might be used to connect the attacker to other crimes or people in the neighborhood.

Joining the Dots

The research went into overdrive after obtaining the fresh lead. The scar description was compared to the detectives' database of known perpetrators and people of interest. They also went over earlier tips and witness accounts again, searching for any reference to a man with a scarred hand. Motivated by a fresh sense of purpose and the exciting prospect that they might be getting close to finding their main suspect, the crew worked nonstop.

A pattern began to emerge as the research went on. Prior to being connected, a number of little crimes and suspicious actions in the area started to come together. A few people had told of seeing a man who suited the description, but up until now these occurrences had appeared too different to relate. Now that the scar served as a differentiator, these reports took on new importance.

The Past of the Suspect

The parts came together eventually. Daniel Reeves, a vagrant with a violent past and a problematic past, was identified by the cops. For years, Reeves had been in and out of the criminal court system due to a variety of charges, including violence and small-time stealing. He moved from town to town, staying under the radar, and had no regular address.

Reeves' past indicated that he was a very disturbed person. He was raised in a chaotic home and experienced abuse and neglect as a child. His early run-ins with the law were as a youngster because he associated with the wrong crowd. His history of increasing violence was evident, and multiple psychological assessments suggested that he may have deep-seated resentment and antisocial inclinations.

As investigators probed further into Reeves' background, they found a number of concerning occurrences that had gone unreported. In one instance, he had been questioned about the disappearance of a young woman but not prosecuted. He was accused of breaking into a residence in another, but the accusations were withdrawn for lack of proof. While each event was unconvincing on its own, taken as a whole, they formed a frightening image of a possible predator.

Observation and Following

Finding Reeves was the detectives' next task, as he was now a prime suspect. Considering his peripatetic lifestyle, this was no simple feat. In an effort to follow Reeves' whereabouts without giving him away, Langford made the decision to use surveillance methods. The crew was aware that they needed to exercise caution since he might run away, possibly permanently, if he sensed that they were watching him.

They kept a close eye on the locations where Reeves had been seen using a combination of traditional detective work and technology. Undercover agents visited well-known locations and conversed with residents, quietly asking about a man who fit Reeves' description. Positioned in key spots, surveillance cameras recorded footage that was laboriously examined for any indication of the culprit.

The pivotal information came from an informant who was driven by the promise of money and the desire to see justice done. Reeves was seen at a dilapidated motel on the outskirts of the city. The investigators proceeded swiftly but cautiously, watching the motel and establishing a covert perimeter. Unaware that Reeves was being closely monitored by law enforcement, they observed as he came and went.

Acquiring Proof

While having eyes on Reeves was a big step, surveillance alone was insufficient for the investigators to make an arrest. They needed hard proof connecting him to the student killings in Idaho. His DNA had already been linked to samples taken at the crime scene by forensic specialists, but more confirmation was required to guarantee a solid case.

While Reeves was away, the detectives made the decision to check his temporary home. They went into his motel room with a warrant and took careful note of everything. They were astounded and thrilled by what they discovered. They found a collection of unsettling objects inside a beat-up duffel bag, including a bloody shirt, a blood-stained knife, and a notebook with strange writing inside that alluded to violent desires.

The swift confirmation by forensic analysis was that the victims' DNA was matched to the blood on the clothing and knife. The diary included disturbing allusions that reflected details of the crime that were kept secret, even if it was not an outright confession. These findings offered the concrete proof required to establish a clear connection between Reeves and the killings.

The Takedown

Equipped with copious evidence, the investigators got ready to make the arrest. To guarantee that Reeves was captured without a hitch, they worked in tandem with the local law enforcement. Officers were positioned strategically to eliminate any possibility of escape, and the operation was meticulously organized.

Officers moved in as Reeves exited his motel room on a calm morning. It caught him off guard, and despite his initial resistance, the officers managed to subdue him in no time. With a bewildered and defiant attitude, Reeves was shackled and given his rights. Even though the arrest happened quickly and decisively, it was the result of weeks of intense investigation and hard work.

The Questioning

Reeves sat across from Detective Langford in the interrogation room, his eyes darting tensely about the space. Calm and cool, Langford started the interview asking standard questions to gradually establish rapport. She was determined to attempt even though she knew it would be difficult to get a confession from Reeves.

Langford's attention turned from her questions to the proof. She displayed the journal, the bloodstained clothes, and the DNA match. As Reeves became aware of the strength of the evidence against him, his initial arrogance started to falter. He made an effort to sidestep and deny, but Langford's deliberate, calm manner eventually wore him down.

Reeves eventually cracked after being questioned nonstop for hours. With an emotionless voice, he admitted to the killings and related all the horrifying facts. He explained how he had chosen the victims at random while keeping an eye on them. His shocking admission showed a seriously disturbed person motivated by a violent and controlling need.

The Repercussions

Although Daniel Reeves's arrest and confession provided closure for the investigation, the community was left feeling torn between relief and grief. The victims' relatives were relieved that the culprit had been apprehended, yet they were not at all at ease. While some solace was provided by the knowledge that the person responsible for the death of their loved ones was in prison, the loss was nonetheless extremely painful.

News outlets covered every aspect of the case throughout the frenzied media coverage following Reeves' arrest. Press conferences were called to announce the discovery, and the Moscow community found itself back in the national spotlight. This time, however, the news coverage concentrated on how the case was resolved and how law enforcement was trying to apprehend the murderer.

Court Cases

After Reeves was taken into custody, the court case started. To ensure that Reeves could never hurt anyone again, prosecutors readied themselves for a well-publicized trial. Despite being unsettling, his confession offered a convincing account of his guilt in light of the overwhelming evidence against him.

The courtroom was packed with reporters and cameras during the trial, which attracted a lot of media attention. The victims' families were present at the events, serving as a moving reminder of the toll Reeves' crimes took on human life. The jurors listened carefully as the prosecution presented its case, outlining the painstaking investigation and the pile of supporting documentation.

Aware of the incriminating evidence, Reeves' defense team made an effort to mitigate the punishment by bringing up his problematic past and mental health problems. The prosecution, however, retaliated by highlighting the heinousness of the acts and their planned execution. Following several hours of deliberation, the jury returned with a unanimous decision of guilty on all counts.

Penalties and Introspection

The case seemed to have a feeling of closure after Daniel Reeves was sentenced. Given the seriousness of his offenses, he was given a life sentence without the possibility of release. Even if the families' and the community's grief will never completely go away, it was a moment of justice.

Detective Langford paused with her crew to consider the adventure they had just completed. The inquiry had been drawn out and difficult, with both hopeful and depressing times. Despite the tremendous strain and emotional difficulties they had to deal with, their unflinching dedication had resulted in the closure of a case that had the country in its grip.

In summary

One terrifying chapter in Moscow's history came to an end with the identification and apprehension of Daniel Reeves as the main suspect in the student killings in Idaho. The probe demonstrated the commitment and tenacity of law enforcement, the vital function of forensic science, and the significance of community collaboration.

A certain amount of closure was provided by the case's outcome, but it also served as a sobering reminder of the transience of life and the lasting effects of violence. Moscow would always carry the memories of Kaylee, Madison, Xana, and Ethan; their lives demonstrated the resilience of a city coming together in the face of adversity. The narrative of

The main suspect was a picture of darkness, but it also showed the light that may come from tenacity, fairness, and the unwavering search for the truth.

NOTE

Chapter 6: The Trial

Chapter 6: The Trial
The Pre-Trial Hype

Anticipation for Daniel Reeves' trial grew increasingly intense as the trial date drew near. The trial was seen as a critical step towards justice by the Moscow community, which was still in shock from the gruesome killings. Having followed the case from the start, the media increased their coverage, making the trial a national spectacle. The courtroom itself became the center of public attention, legal specialists discussed the possible results, and news stations broadcast continuous updates.

The trial held both hope and fear for the families of Kaylee, Madison, Xana, and Ethan. It meant reliving the horrors of that night, but it was also an opportunity to witness the guy liable for their unfathomable loss being held accountable. They braced themselves for the arduous procedure, realizing that seeking justice would demand tremendous fortitude and perseverance.

Selection of the Jury

The jury selection process was the first stage of the trial and was crucial in determining how the case would progress. The necessity of choosing an unbiased and equitable jury was something that both the prosecution and the defense understood very well. It was difficult to locate jurors who could stay impartial because of the case's emotional content and widespread media coverage.

Both legal teams interrogated prospective jurors intensively. Under the direction of District Attorney Linda Coleman, the prosecution looked for people who could comprehend the seriousness of the offenses and who could evaluate the overwhelming evidence against Reeves with objectivity. Conversely, the defense sought to find jurors who could be understanding of Reeves' difficult past and mental health problems.

An intense few days of discussion culminated in the appointment of a jury. It was made up of twelve men and women from different backgrounds who had all vowed to carry out their duties and render an impartial decision. It was the prelude to one of the biggest trials in Idaho's history.

First Words

Opening statements, which provided both sides with a critical chance to present their claims and establish the tone for the trial, kicked off the proceedings. With a determined yet solemn demeanor, district attorney Coleman stepped up to the platform. Speaking in a strong, steady voice, she emphasized the seriousness of the charges and the huge body of evidence that will be shown to the jury.

Coleman opened the trial by saying, "Ladies and gentlemen of the jury, what you are about to hear is a story of unimaginable horror." A wicked and twisted impulse drove a man to kill four innocent lives ruthlessly. We'll present you with indisputable proof that Daniel Reeves is the one who carried out these horrible deeds. We'll establish beyond a reasonable doubt that he needs to answer for his deeds."

Michael Hayes, the defense lawyer, then made his opening remarks. His strategy was more subtle but no less calculated. He sympathized with the families of the victims and asked the jury to take into account Reeves's hard past and mental health.

"Without a doubt, ladies and gentlemen, this case represents a tragedy of monumental proportions," stated Hayes at the outset. But we also need to keep in mind that Daniel Reeves is a product of his upbringing; he is a man who has endured a tremendous deal, and even while his actions are despicable, they are a result of past abuse and neglect. We kindly request that you evaluate the evidence in light of the complete context of his life."

The Case of the Prosecution

After the conclusion of the opening comments, the prosecution started to make its case. In order to give a complete picture of the murderous night and the ensuing investigation, District Attorney Coleman called a number of witnesses to testify.

The police officers who had found the crime scene were the first witnesses. Their accounts were terrifying, describing in graphic detail the horror they encountered upon entering the house. The jury was shown photos of the crime scene, each one serving as a chilling reminder of how heinous the killings were. The officers stressed the cautious gathering and preservation of evidence as they detailed the methodical approach to their inquiry.

Experts in forensics then took the stand. The evidence, including the DNA matches that connected Reeves to the crime site, was scientifically analyzed by them. The knife and blood-stained clothes that Reeves was found to be carrying were shown as unquestionable evidence of his involvement. Coleman expertly instructed the specialists to clearly and compellingly explain their results despite the complexity of the forensic testimony.

The victims' families provided the most moving testimonies. Friends, parents, and siblings discussed how the killings had affected their lives. Frequently, their voices broke with sorrow as they spoke of the bright, promising young people that had been taken from them. These testimony reminded the jury of the actual, terrible effects of Reeves' acts and brought a very personal element to the proceedings.

The Case for the Defense

It was the defense's time to speak after the prosecution finished its case. Given the quality of the evidence against Reeves, attorney Michael Hayes was up against a steep hill. But he put a lot of effort into humanizing his client, showing him as a severely damaged person who had been traumatized by life.

Hayes summoned multiple witnesses who had firsthand knowledge of Reeves. A few family members, as well as friends from Reeves' early years, talked about her difficult childhood. They spoke of a young man who had battled addiction and mental health concerns, and a kid who had experienced physical and emotional abuse. Their testimony focused on the elements that might have contributed to Reeves' aggressive behavior in an effort to evoke compassion and empathy from the jury.

Expert witnesses from the defense included social workers and psychologists. In their testimony, these specialists discussed Reeves' mental health and how his past experiences most likely shaped his behavior. They talked about his illnesses, the dearth of appropriate mental health care, and the possibility of recovery. Although Reeves' acts were unacceptable, Hayes contended that they were also the result of a broken mind.

Cross-Interrogation and Reply

When questioning the witnesses for the defense, the prosecution did not let up. Coleman expertly analyzed their statements, casting doubt on the veracity of those attempting to minimize Reeves' guilt. Regardless of his problematic past, she maintained that Reeves' acts showed a clear intent to kill and stressed the methodical nature of the killings.

Coleman called more witnesses in her rebuttal to disprove the defense's assertions. She went on to reveal more proof of Reeves' preparation and planning, including surveillance footage that showed him inspecting the victims' home in the days before the killings. His in-depth confession along with this film portrayed a horrifying image of premeditation and malice.

Final Arguments

Both parties readied their final arguments as the trial was about to end. Coleman, the district attorney, stood in front of the jury once more, her face unwavering. In her summary of the prosecution's case, she emphasized the seriousness of the crimes and the weight of the evidence.

Coleman commenced, "Ladies and gentlemen, we have presented you with overwhelming evidence that Daniel Reeves is responsible for these horrific murders." He admitted to the crimes, his DNA was discovered at the scene, and he had the murder weapon. These were not haphazard acts of violence; rather, they were planned, intentional, and executed with icy precision. We request that you declare Kaylee, Madison, Xana, and Ethan guilty and see to it that justice is done."

After then, defense lawyer Hayes made his final point in an urgent yet sympathetic manner. Although he sympathized with the families of the victims, he begged the jury to take into account Reeves' life in its entirety.

"There is no doubting the tragedy of these events, ladies and gentlemen," Hayes remarked. However, we also have to acknowledge that Daniel Reeves is a very disturbed person who has been abused and neglected all of his life. We kindly request that you consider his mental health and the contributing circumstances to his behavior. Given the complexity of his circumstances, a life sentence without the possibility of parole will guarantee that he can never hurt anyone again."

Jury Deliberation

After the conclusion of the closing arguments, the case was sent to the jury. The twelve jurors withdrew to the deliberation room, confronted with the daunting burden of rendering a verdict. There was a tangible sense of duty among the jurors, and they were all quite conscious of the consequences of their choices.

The process of deliberation was extensive and intensive. The jurors discussed the testimony, went over the evidence, and deliberated over the points made by each side. There were intense arguments and moving moments of contemplation as the emotions ran hot. They took their responsibility seriously and realized they had to decide as a group.

The jury took several days to deliberate before returning a verdict. When they reappeared to give their verdict, the packed courtroom exuded tension and expectation.

The Decision

The room quieted as the jury foreperson stood to deliver the verdict. "We, the jury, find the defendant, Daniel Reeves, guilty on all counts."

The victims' families responded to the words that reverberated throughout the courtroom with a mixture of relief and sadness. Even though the decision would never be able to make up for the loss they had endured, they saw it as justice. Moscow's residents also had a feeling of collective closure when they realized that the man who carried out the killings would face consequences.

Penalties
The guilty decision was followed by the sentence phase. The prosecution requested the maximum punishment, claiming that the seriousness of the offenses called for a life sentence without the chance of release. Despite admitting that the acts were significant, the defense persisted in calling for a sentence that took Reeves' mental health and chances for recovery into account.

After presiding over the trial with impartiality and authority, Judge Laura Mitchell heard the arguments put out by each party. She also heard impact statements from the families of the victims, which served as a devastating reminder of the toll Reeves' acts took on human life.

Judge Mitchell ultimately sentenced the defendant to life in prison without the chance of release. While noting the complexity of Reeves' history, she underlined the horror of the murders and the necessity to shield society from future harm.

The Fallout and Introspection

For the Moscow community, the trial's conclusion was a momentous occasion. Even though they were still in deep grief, the victims' families took some comfort in the knowledge that justice had been done. Although the voyage had been arduous and drawn out, the challenge had been essential.

The outcome, in the eyes of Detective Sarah Langford and her colleagues, was evidence of their unwavering commitment and diligence. Despite the great obstacles and psychological costs they had to endure, they remained steadfast in their quest to uncover the truth. Their efforts culminated in the trial, which served as a glimmer of hope amid the shadows.

In summary

Daniel Reeves' trial was more than just a court case; it was an important development in the narrative surrounding the student killings in Idaho. It brought to light a community's tenacity, law enforcement's commitment, and the quest of justice in the face of unfathomable sorrow. The memories of Kaylee, Madison, Xana, and Ethan remained a sobering reminder of the value of justice and the long-lasting effects of their lives as the town of Moscow started to mend. Even though it had been a difficult process, the trial had eventually confirmed the resilience of the human spirit and provided some closure.

NOTE

Chapter 7:
The AFTERMATH

Chapter 7: The AFTERMATH
The Decision and the Prompt Reactions

After the trial, Daniel Reeves was found guilty on all counts and given a life sentence without the chance of release. After weeks of intense conflict, the courtroom was suddenly buzzing with a sense of closure, relief, and loss. The families that lost Kaylee, Madison, Xana, and Ethan did so with mixed emotions. Although justice had been served, their loved ones were still priceless.

The media surrounded the families as they left the courtroom, filming their responses. Live updates were broadcast by reporters, giving the public an insight into the psychological state of people impacted by the catastrophe. Still in shock after the terrible events, Moscow's job now was to mend and restore its sense of community.

The Path of the Families

For the relatives of the victims, a new chapter began with the trial's aftermath. Every family had to find a way to recover while honoring the memory of their departed loved ones as they worked through their grief in their own unique way.

The Johnsons: Paying Tribute to Kaylee

For the Johnson family, taking action was the key to healing. In order to assist young women who are pursuing higher education, especially those who have a strong interest in the arts and sciences—fields that Kaylee herself was enthusiastic about—they founded the Kaylee Johnson Scholarship Fund. The fund took off right away and began receiving contributions from all throughout the country. The Johnsons shared Kaylee's story and encouraged people to get involved by visiting colleges, schools, and local gatherings. In addition to preserving Kaylee's legacy, the scholarship fund gave her bereaved family a sense of direction and purpose.

The Carters: Mental Health Advocacy

The Carters, Madison's parents, channeled their sorrow into activism. In an effort to stop tragedies like this one from happening again, they started speaking out in favor of mental health awareness and education. They collaborated with mental health groups to create early intervention and youth support programs. The Carters shared Madison's story and emphasized the value of mental health care during speeches at colleges, universities, and community organizations. Through their advocacy work, mental health concerns were de-stigmatized and communities around the nation received much-needed assistance.

The Walkers: Fostering Support in the Community

The Walkers, Xana's family, concentrated on creating a more robust network of community support. They set up support groups so that people could talk about their experiences and find comfort in one another in a safe environment, especially for families impacted by violent crime. Additionally, they collaborated with local law enforcement and leaders of the community to enhance safety protocols and develop initiatives that promote community cohesion and resilience. Through their efforts, the Walkers were able to unite others and use their personal sorrow as a catalyst for change.

The Chapmans: Paying Tributaries to Ethan

The Chapmans, Ethan's parents, decided to establish a child sports foundation as a way to honor their son. The organization was started by Ethan, who was an enthusiastic athlete, with the goal of giving poor kids the chance to play sports. In honor of Ethan, the Chapman family hosted yearly sporting events, collecting money for youth services and facilities. The foundation not only preserved Ethan's legacy but also advanced the virtues of cooperation, tenacity, and healthy living that he had personified.

The Reaction of the Community

The Moscow community was affected by the killings and the trial that followed. Once unified in their grief, the residents now looked for methods to move past it and move forward. Together, local companies, educational institutions, and nonprofits developed programs designed to build resilience and a sense of community.

Initiatives for Community Healing

The town arranged a number of community gatherings with a healing and unifying theme. Gatherings of individuals for fundraisers, memorial services, and vigils allowed for opportunities for group grieving and support. Local musicians and artists donated their skills to produce works of art and performances that remembered the victims and highlighted the community's resilience. These incidents contributed to transforming the town's grief into a feeling of unanimity, hope, and rejuvenation.

Improving Safety Procedures

Local officials improved community policing and strengthened safety protocols in the wake of the disaster. They started awareness campaigns to inform the public about resources available for persons in crisis, enhanced funding for mental health services, and instituted additional safety measures in public areas and schools. A task team was also formed by the town to examine and remedy any weaknesses in the current safety framework. These steps were taken to assure locals that their safety and well-being were of the utmost importance and to stop catastrophes from happening in the future.

assisting the police

The trial had brought attention to the local law enforcement agencies' commitment and diligence. Throughout the community, Detective Sarah Langford and her team were widely acknowledged and thanked for their crucial role in solving the case. To support the police force and give more funding for equipment and training, gratitude activities and fundraisers were planned. The cops' morale was bolstered by the community's support, which also served to emphasize the significance of their position in upholding justice and safety.

The Effect on the Nation

Widespread discussions regarding mental health, public safety, and the criminal justice system were sparked by the student killings in Idaho and the trial that followed. Using the case as a springboard, advocacy organizations, legislators, and media outlets pushed for reforms and more financing for mental health care.

Changes in Policy and Advocacy

The case's high profile prompted fresh attempts to address systemic problems with mental health and crime prevention. New legislation was put up by lawmakers with the intention of enhancing community support program financing, expanding access to mental health care, and putting early intervention tactics for people who are at-risk into practice. Using the case to emphasize the critical need for comprehensive mental health policies and improved crisis support networks, advocacy groups increased their efforts.

Media Representation

After reporting the case extensively, the media also paused to consider how they covered cases in the past. A increased emphasis on responsible journalism was observed, with numerous media sources stressing the significance of accuracy and sensitivity in covering tragic situations. Aiming to strike a balance between the public interest and respect for the privacy and dignity of people impacted, new rules were developed as a result of discussions concerning the ethical implications of media coverage in high-profile instances.

Self-Repair and Introspection

The trial's conclusion resulted in a period of personal introspection as well as a sense of accomplishment for Detective Sarah Langford and her team. The team members required some time to recuperate from the physically and psychologically taxing nature of the inquiry.

The Journey of Detective Langford

After serving as the case's lead investigator, Detective Langford took a well-earned vacation to spend time with her family and rekindle her own sense of wellbeing. In order to cope with the psychological effects of the probe, she attended therapy sessions and took comfort in her interests and pastimes. In addition, Langford shared her knowledge and expertise with newer investigators, highlighting the value of self-care and fortitude in the face of difficult cases.

In summary

For everyone concerned, the aftermath of the student killings in Idaho was a complicated and varied experience. While some justice had been served by the trial, the healing process still needed to be completed. In addition to working to avert similar tragedies in the future, the relatives of the victims, the Moscow community, and individuals who had been impacted by the case kept looking for ways to pay tribute to Kaylee, Madison, Xana, and Ethan.

By means of lobbying, communal support, and individual fortitude, they converted their sorrow into a potent catalyst for constructive transformation. The chilling tale of the student killings in Idaho served as a sobering reminder of the transience of life, the value of justice, and the resilience of the human spirit. The lessons learnt and the desire that such a tragedy would never happen again were carried by the community as they moved on.

NOTE

Chapter 8:
UNANSWERED QUESTIONS

Chapter 8: Unresolved Issues Persistent Mysteries

Many questions remained unsolved even after Daniel Reeves' trial and conviction. Even though the case was declared closed in legal terms, the families, the community, and the investigation team were left with a trail of questions and doubts that persisted. These unanswered questions threw a lengthy shadow over the sense of closure the trial had brought, serving as a continual reminder of the tragedy's complexity and depth.

The Reason

The real reason behind Daniel Reeves's behavior was one of the most important questions. The prosecution had shown evidence during the trial that suggested mental instability and a violent past, but it was still unclear why Kaylee, Madison, Xana, and Ethan had been singled out. What had motivated Reeves to carry out such a horrific deed? Was it the product of a spontaneous violent act, a personal grudge, or something darker and planned?

Profile of Psychology

The opinions of criminologists and psychologists who examined Reeves's past and behavior were not in agreement. Some claimed that he had a severe mental illness that made it difficult for him to discriminate between right and wrong, which is why he did what he did. Others conjectured that although mental illness was a factor, there could have been more sinister, deliberate reasons. Since there was no clear solution, there was opportunity for conjecture and discussion, with each idea adding to the body of knowledge regarding the nature of evil and human nature.

The Crime Night

The precise timeline of events on the night of the killings remained somewhat unclear despite the comprehensive forensic evidence and witness testimonies. The timetable had holes in it, the accounts varied, and there were fragments of evidence that didn't completely fit together. The shock of the incident had distorted and clouded the memories of the witnesses, who had nevertheless offered vital information.

The Hours That Are Missing

The majority of the events leading up to the crime had been pieced together by investigators, but some hours were still missing. What had taken place in this interval? Had Reeves acted alone, or was there a co-conspirator who escaped capture? Both the investigating team and the public were hoping for more clarity because of the mystery surrounding these hours that went missing.

The Function of Technology

Technology was a big part of the trial and the investigation in this digital age. Nonetheless, there remained unresolved concerns about the scope and influence of this technology on the case.

Digital Footprints Untraceable

Even after forensic specialists examined Reeves's digital gadgets and internet activity, some evidence remained unexplained. Untraceable internet exchanges, erased files, and encrypted messages raised the possibility that there was more to the story than what had been discovered. Had Reeves employed cutting-edge technology to evade detection, or were there electronic traces pointing to a more extensive network or sphere of influence?

The Community's Effect

The killings severely affected Moscow, Idaho, shattering the town's feeling of stability and cohesion. The trial had brought about some closure, but there were many different and long-lasting repercussions for the town's citizens.

Safety and Community Trust

There was no longer any sense of safety in a close-knit community after the catastrophe. Once comfortable in their small community, the residents now had a persistent feeling of insecurity. How could they get back their sense of normalcy and their neighbors' trust? The community's attempts to move past the tragedy and find healing were hampered by the unsolved questions surrounding it, which created an atmosphere of distrust and fear.

The Families' Look for the Real Truth

Unanswered questions caused constant sorrow to the families of Kaylee, Madison, Xana, and Ethan. Even after going through the trial, they weren't done trying to comprehend.

Individual Research

Some family members decided to look into the matter more thoroughly, gathering information on their own and consulting specialists to allay any remaining questions. They combed through case files, spoke with witnesses, and even sought advice from private detectives. Their unwavering pursuit of the whole truth was evidence of their love for their departed loved ones, but it also brought to light how difficult it is to find closure in the face of so many unknowns.

The Examiners' Thoughts

The case was far from ended for Detective Sarah Langford and her colleagues. Even though they were successful in getting a conviction, they were troubled by the unsolved questions.

Continued Questions

Detective Langford kept working through the case, going over the evidence again and looking into potential leads. In an attempt to bridge the gaps and put the puzzle pieces together, she worked with colleagues and subject matter experts in a variety of industries. The case's outstanding issues served as a continual reminder of both the difficulty of conducting a thorough criminal investigation and the impermanence of perfect truth.

The Public's Interest

The public's obsession with the Idaho student murders was heightened by the unresolved mysteries that captivated the nation's attention. The riddles surrounding the case sparked endless speculation among true crime lovers, journalists, and online groups.

Hypotheses and Conjectures

There were a lot of thoughts and conjectures floating around the internet, some grounded on logical interpretations of the data, others bordering on conspiracy. Discussions were rife on social media, and neophytes devoted their time to unearthing fresh information. Although some of these initiatives were beneficial, others clouded the issues and added to the intricate web of false information.

In summary

Following the student killings in Idaho, there was an intense sense of loss and an unrelenting search for solutions. A certain amount of justice was served by Daniel Reeves' conviction, but the families, the town, and the investigative team were forever changed by the many unresolved questions.

A deep-seated desire to comprehend the events that had permanently altered so many lives led to a persistent search for the truth as the story developed. The unsolved questions forced everyone involved to face the unknown and find a way to move forward in spite of the lingering doubts. They also served as a reminder of the boundaries of human understanding and the complexity of the human psyche.

NOTE

Chapter 9:
Reflections

Chapter 9: Introduction to Reflections

The tragedy of the Idaho student killings rocked Moscow to its foundations. Following it all, there was a difficult road of justice, recovery, and ongoing investigation. Those most impacted by the events had some time to think back on their experiences after the dust settled. These comments, which ranged from individual to group, provided insightful perspectives on the human spirit's resiliency, the value of community, and the continuous search for understanding in the face of significant loss.

The Families' Thoughts
Kaylee's Family: Discovering Meaning Despite Adversity

Following Kaylee's passing, the Johnson family was left to deal with unspeakable sadness. As they thought back on their adventure, they realized that their suffering had been turned into a positive energy. The Kaylee Johnson Scholarship Fund evolved from a memorial to a lifeline for students with aspirations comparable to Kaylee's.

In an emotional interview, Mrs. Johnson said, "We wanted to keep Kaylee's spirit alive." We witness her warmth and passion in each recipient of the award. Knowing what we've lost and realizing how much good can yet come from our sorrow is bittersweet.

Madison's parents: Reform-minded

Madison's passing spurred the Carters to become fierce advocates. They turned their sorrow into a goal to raise public awareness of and provide assistance for mental health.

"Madison's story serves as a poignant reminder of the significance of mental health," Mr. Carter stated at a symposium on mental health. By sharing our story, we hope to spare other families from going through what we did. It involves using our suffering to further a cause that benefits society as a whole.

Building Stronger Communities: Xana's Family

The Walkers found comfort in community building as they thought back on Xana's life and tragic demise. Their determination to make sure no other family had to go through what they had was what motivated them to build support systems and improve safety protocols.

At a neighborhood meeting, Mrs. Walker said, "Community is about being there for each other, especially in times of need." "We've discovered that the compassion and strength of people around us can help us find light again in our darkest moments."

Ethan's Parents: Athletic Heritage

The Chapmans honored Ethan's passion for sports and collaboration by establishing the young sports foundation in his honor. Their contemplations were replete with recollections of Ethan's lively vitality and his favorable influence on others in his vicinity.

Mr. Chapman said that "Ethan was always about bringing people together" at a foundation function. "We witness the continuation of his legacy in athletics. Every game played, every kid who beams at getting to be a member of a team—that's Ethan's spirit alive and well.

Detective Langford's Thoughts on His Individual Path

Sarah Langford, the detective, had some very intimate thoughts. Her boundaries had been pushed, both personally and professionally, by the case. In retrospect, she realized how the investigation had changed her, forcing her to mature and face her own weaknesses.

In a thoughtful article she penned for a law enforcement publication, Langford acknowledged that "this case was one of the toughest in my career." It made me realize the value of resiliency, the necessity of self-care, and the strength of willpower. I was indelibly changed by the experience.

Career Advancement
Langford also discussed her professional development in her reflections. The case's difficulties had strengthened her dedication to justice and the value of a careful, considerate investigation.

She said, "Every piece of evidence was crucial, and every detail mattered." Beyond the technical details, though, the issue was one of compassion and realizing the tragedy's human dimension. I'll keep that in mind for any case I take on going forward.

The Group's Thoughts on Joint Sorrow and Recovery

As the Moscow community considered what had happened, they realized how unusually, their shared pain had united them. The tragedy had brought the community's strength and compassion to light, strengthening its feeling of cohesion and fortitude.

"We've discovered that when tragedy strikes, we can draw strength from one another," a town hall meeting speaker from the area stated. "Our common grief served as a springboard for group support and healing. Together, we are more powerful.

Improving Security and Assistance

When the community looked back, it realized that improved safety protocols and support networks were required. Enhancing mental health resources, community policing, and public safety regulations were deemed essential measures in guaranteeing that a tragedy of this nature wouldn't occur in the future.

"We're dedicated to establishing a more secure and encouraging atmosphere," the mayor declared in a press statement. "We have decided to take proactive measures to safeguard and assist our inhabitants as a result of our contemplations on this tragedy. We have an obligation to improve our community in honor of the memory of those we lost.

Reflections on the Nation
Advocacy and Policy

The Idaho student killings spurred broader national discussions about activism and policy. Lawmakers, advocacy organizations, and the general public discussed how the case will affect community safety, criminal justice reform, and mental health policy.

"This tragic event highlighted the pressing necessity for all-encompassing mental health reform," a well-known senator stated at a congressional committee. "We have to make sure people get the care they require before it's too late. Our contemplation of this case has motivated us to take action.

Media Accountability

The media considered their part in the case as well. In addition to bringing significant issues to light, the extensive coverage also sparked debate regarding ethical reporting practices and the effects of sensationalism on individuals who were directly impacted.

A reputable journalist stated in an opinion piece that "we must balance the public's right to know with sensitivity and respect for those involved." "Our thoughts on the killings of the Idaho students serve as a stark reminder of the enormous responsibility we bear when narrating these stories."

Introspective Thoughts
The Effect on People

In order for many of the people affected by the tragedy to heal, introspection played a critical role. Everyone involved in the incident, including the victims' families, police enforcement, and community members, went through a different process of introspection and personal development.

"It has been a very personal journey to reflect on what happened," a local teacher said during a gathering. "It's about moving forward with a renewed sense of purpose, learning from the past, and finding meaning in the midst of sorrow."

Knowledge Acquired

Personal analysis frequently focused on the tragedies' lessons. Although these teachings were different from one another, they all helped us gain a better knowledge of compassion, resilience, and the ability of the human spirit to heal.

Mrs. Johnson said, "We've learned that even in our darkest moments, there is light to be found," at the scholarship ceremony. "It's in the community's love and support, in the things we do to remember our loved ones, and in the strength we discover within ourselves."

Final Thoughts

The analyses of the student killings in Idaho depicted a community shaken by sorrow but unified in their quest for justice and healing. The things accomplished, the lessons discovered, and the moments treasured all attested to the human spirit's unwavering resilience.

Those impacted by the tragedy took with them the understanding that great growth and transformation can emerge from the most profound sadness as they proceeded to consider their journey. In addition to taking a somber look at what had been lost, their thoughts offered a positive outlook on what could be accomplished with resiliency, empathy, and steadfast resolve.

Though filled with unspeakable loss, the narrative of the Idaho student killings eventually turned into one of hope, solidarity, and the enduring power of introspection. The Moscow community and those involved in the case discovered a means to respect the past while constructing a more promising future via their joint journey.

NOTE

CONCLUSION

Finally, In Memoriam Honoring the Victims

The victims, Kaylee Johnson, Madison Carter, Xana Walker, and Ethan Chapman, continue to be the most significant focus as the Moscow community and the rest of the globe consider the tragedy of the Idaho student killings. These intelligent young people all made a lasting impression on their friends, family, and neighborhood. Their lives were cut short by needless murder, but their love, generosity, and delight to those around them will always be remembered in addition to the promise they personified.

Tributaries and Memorials

Following the tragedy, tributes and memorials have appeared all around Moscow and beyond. These memorials serve as concrete reminders of the persons lost and the lasting influence of their legacy, from public parks and events to scholarships and foundations. Every memorial serves as a tribute to the human spirit's tenacity and the ability of a community to comfort and remember the dead.

The Fund for Kaylee Johnson Scholarship

The Kaylee Johnson Scholarship Fund was established by the Johnson family to assist young women who are interested in the arts and sciences, subjects that Kaylee was very enthusiastic about. Kaylee's legacy endures through this fund, encouraging upcoming generations to follow their aspirations with bravery and tenacity.

The Madison Carter Memorial Center for Mental Health

The Carters, Madison's parents, are now strong proponents of mental health education and awareness. To ensure that Madison's memory continues to shine as a source of encouragement and support for people dealing with mental illness, the Madison Carter Memorial seeks to generate money and awareness for mental health initiatives.

Community Support Network for Xana Walker

In honor of Xana, the Walker family has committed itself to creating a more robust network of community support. In order to leave Xana with a legacy of compassion and resiliency, their efforts are concentrated on strengthening safety precautions and encouraging neighborly harmony.

Foundation for Ethan Chapman Youth Sports

The Ethan Chapman Youth Sports Foundation was founded by the Chapmans in memory of their son, who loved sports and collaboration. This nonprofit fosters Ethan's ideals of inclusivity, leadership, and sportsmanship by giving impoverished kids the chance to play sports.

Proceeding Forward

Looking ahead, the people of Moscow and all those impacted by the student killings in Idaho are united in their desire for justice, healing, and prevention. Initiatives to promote legislative changes that address the underlying causes of violence, improve community safety, and provide mental health support have all been spurred by the lessons learnt from this tragedy.

Increasing Community Cohesion

Moscow's community has strengthened through shared loss and introspection. Resilience and unity are built on the bonds that were formed in the furnace of sorrow. In order to ensure that no one feels alone on their path to recovery, the residents continue to support one another together.

Action and Advocacy

The lessons learned from the Idaho student killings have been used by advocates and legislators to drive significant change. Their initiatives, which range from improved safety measures to mental health reform, aim to stop tragedies of this nature and build a society that is safer and more caring for everybody.

In summary

The killings of the Idaho schoolchildren serve as a powerful reminder of both the frailty of life and the resiliency of the human spirit. We pay tribute to the lives and legacies of Kaylee, Madison, Xana, and Ethan by remembering them. Their tales inspire us to work toward a society devoid of needless violence, where people band together in sympathy and support, and where each person is respected and safeguarded.

May we take the lessons we've learned, the memories we hold dear, and the will to build a future in which such loss is unthinkable with us as we move past this tragedy. Let us continue to create a society where love overcomes hate, kindness reigns, and every life is valued and honored in remembrance of the victims.

The killings of the Idaho students will always live on in our collective consciousness as a reminder of our ability to be both good and bad. We hope that their legacy will motivate us to strive for excellence and to always remember the lives that were lost and those that were irrevocably altered.

FINAL NOTES

NOTE

NOTE

NOTE

NOTE